Shetland Ponies Are My Favorite!

Elaine Landau

LERNER PUBLICATIONS COMPANY · MINNEAPOLIS

Lerner Publications Company
A division of Lerner Publishing Group, Inc.
241 First Avenue North
Minneapolis, MN 55401 U.S.A.

Website address: www.lernerbooks.com

Library of Congress Cataloging-in-Publication Data

Landau, Elaine.
    Shetland ponies are my favorite! / by Elaine Landau.
       p.   cm. — (My favorite horses)
    Includes index.
    ISBN 978-0-7613-6534-1 (lib. bdg. : alk. paper)
    1. Shetland pony—Juvenile literature. I. Title.
  SF315.2.S5L36 2012
  636.1′6—dc22   2011011660

Manufactured in the United States of America
1 – PP – 12/31/11

PHOTO ACKNOWLEDGEMENTS

The images in this book are used with the permission of: © Sabine Stuewer/www.
kimballstock.com, pp. 3, 20; © Mindbodysoul/SuperStock, p. 4; © F1 Online/
SuperStock, p. 6; © Redmond Durrell/Alamy, p. 7; © Only Horses TbK/Alamy, p. 8; ©
Thomas Northcut/Digital Vision/Getty Images, p. 9 (top); © Wildlife GmbH/Alamy,
p. 9 (bottom); © Darlene Wohlart, pp. 10-11; © Shetland Museum Photographic
Archive, pp. 12, 13; © Keystone Archives/Heritage-Images/Glow Images, p. 14; © Mira
Oberman/AFP/Getty Images, p. 15; © Animals Animals/SuperStock, p. 16; © Fiona
Green, pp. 17, 18; © Image Source/Getty Images, p. 19; © Kit Houghton/CORBIS, p. 21;
© Biosphoto/Stoelwinder, p. 22.

Front Cover: © Patrick Dieudonne/Robert Harding World Imagery /Getty Images.
Back Cover: © Mike Dunning/Dorling Kindersley /Getty Images.

Main body text set in Atelier Sans ITC Std 16/24.
Typeface provided by International Typeface Corp.

TABLE OF CONTENTS

WHAT A PONY!

Do you long to own a pony?

If you do, I know one you'd really like. You may have seen it at fairs and petting zoos. You might have even ridden it. This adorable animal is one of the best-liked ponies in the country. It's a Shetland!

No one can argue that Shetlands make great pets. But can you *really* get one? Or have your parents said no to keeping such a big animal? Even if that's the case, you don't have to give up your passion for ponies. You can still learn all about the Shetland. Besides, who knows? Maybe someday when you're grown up, you'll own one after all!

Chapter One

MEET THE SHETLAND PONY

It's easy to see why Shetlands are beloved. These ponies are cuties for sure. They also have sweet personalities. Shetlands are just plain fun to have around.

Shetland Body Type

Shetlands are solidly built. They have small, broad heads and stocky bodies. Their legs are short and strong. Shetlands also have long, full manes and bushy tails. They grow a thick double coat in the winter.

Did You Know?

Animals that grow double coats have two layers of fur. One layer is short and lies close to the animal's skin. The other layer is long and grows over the shorter layer.

Size and Color

Shetlands are the perfect size for kids to ride. They are usually about 44 inches (112 centimeters) tall. That's just a little bit bigger than a very large dog. Shetlands can be almost any color. One of the most common colors is black. Many Shetlands are also brown, gray, bay (deep red), and chestnut (dark reddish brown).

The Perfect Pony

Shetland ponies are good natured and very smart. They are gentle and easy to train. Their owners often call them the perfect pony!

A horse and a Shetland pony stand next to each other. You can see how large the horse is compared to the little Shetland.

Ponies and Horses: What's the Difference?

Do you know the difference between a pony and a horse? Ponies and horses are the same species, or type of animal—so they share a lot in common. But height is one difference between the two. Horses are usually 58 inches (147 cm) tall or taller. Ponies are shorter than 58 inches. Ponies also have more fur than horses. A horse's mane, tail, and coat are thinner than a pony's. In addition, ponies and horses have different body shapes. A pony's body tends to be quite wide for its size. A horse's body is typically long and lean.

Pony Diagram

You know that ponies have a mane, a tail, and four hooves. But can you find a pony's flank? Or its fetlock? Let's take a closer look at a pony. Soon you'll be an expert on all the parts that make up these terrific animals.

croup

back

dock

tail

flank

thigh

hock

barrel

fetlock

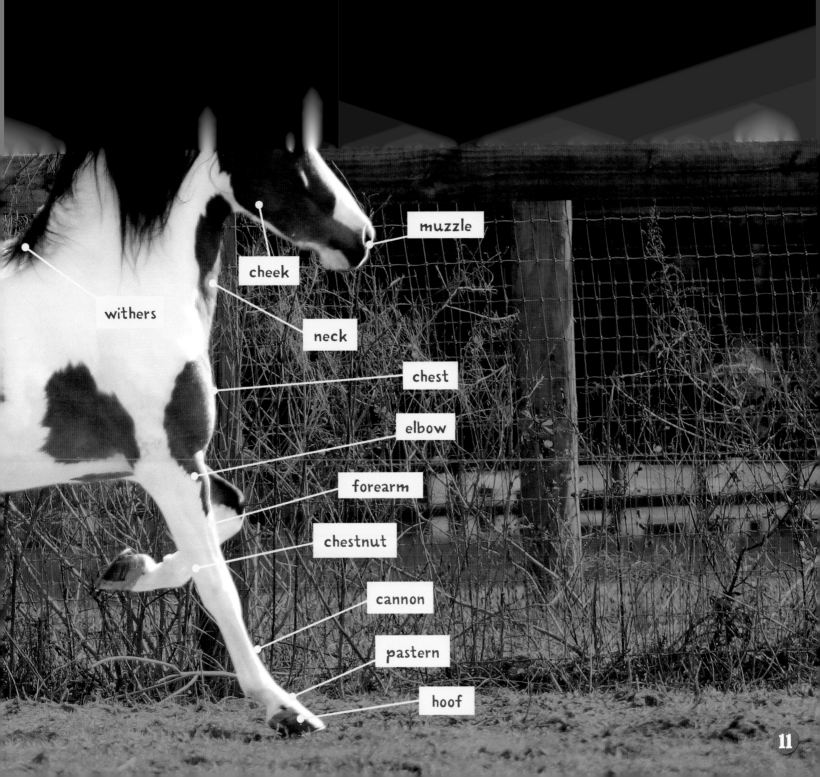

withers

muzzle

cheek

neck

chest

elbow

forearm

chestnut

cannon

pastern

hoof

Chapter Two
THE SHETLAND'S PAST

The Shetland pony comes from the Shetland Islands. These islands are off the northern coast of Scotland. It's very cold and windy there. The Shetland had to be a strong breed to survive.

A Shetland pony lies in some straw in a field on a Shetland island.

The islanders made good use of Shetland ponies. The animals plowed farmland and pulled carts. They also carried heavy loads of coal and peat (partly decayed plant matter), which the islanders burned for fuel.

A Hard Life

Pit ponies faced many hardships. Their hours were long, and their work was difficult. Most ponies rarely got to leave the mines. They spent very little time in the sun.

Yet pit ponies worked hard at their jobs. They did work that human miners couldn't do. Pit ponies helped mine far more coal than humans could have mined alone.

In the mid-1800s, many Shetland ponies were brought to England. They worked as pit ponies there. Pit ponies hauled coal in mines. The Shetland's small size made it perfect for this job. It could easily move through narrow mine tunnels. Some Shetlands were also sent to the United States to work in mines.

A Popular Pony

These days, children often ride Shetland ponies for pleasure. You can also see them in parades and petting zoos. Some Shetlands have been trained as guide ponies. Guide ponies lead blind people to wherever they need to go.

The Shetland pony can do lots of jobs well. But whatever job it does, one thing is certain: it brings plenty of joy to all those who work with it!

This pony guides a blind student to class.

Chapter Three

THE REAL DEAL

Would having a Shetland pony be a dream come true? Think hard before you answer. A pony may be a wonderful pet. Yet ponies are also a lot of work.

A Pad Fit for a Pony

Your pony would need a home. A pony isn't small enough to stay in your bedroom. Do you live on a farm or a ranch? Then your pony could stay in a fenced-in pasture. It would also need some type of shelter. This could be a sturdy, three-sided shelter to protect your pony when the weather is bad.

You'd be spending a lot of your time in the pasture too. A pony needs to be fed and brushed daily. You'd also have to remove its manure, or droppings, from the pasture.

Stable Life

Another choice is to board your pony at a stable. The crew there could care for it. This is known as full board. Full board makes things much easier for a pony owner. But it costs a lot. Many people can't afford it.

You can care for your own pony at a stable as well. This would mean you'd have to go to the stable daily. It would be your job to feed, groom, and exercise your pony. You'd also have to remove the manure from its stall.

Tidy Tack

There's still more pony owners have to do. They have to care for their pony's tack, or gear. Caring for tack is a big job. A pony's saddle, reins, bridle, and other items need to be washed weekly.

This girl makes sure to wash her pony's saddle every week.

Let's Ride

Think there's only one way to ride a pony? Think again! Different styles of riding exist. The two main styles are called English and Western.

English riders hold the reins with both hands. They use a lightweight saddle that has a nearly flat seat. Western riders hold the reins with one hand. Their saddles have a high front and back. They also have a horn.

Other Ways to Enjoy Ponies

Is owning a pony much more work than you thought? It can be quite a task. But don't give up on Shetlands just yet. You don't have to own a Shetland to enjoy them. Here are other fun things you can do.

Make ponies your hobby.
Read up on the Shetland. Find any books, magazines, and DVDs about it. There may be YouTube videos on these appealing ponies too. Become a young expert on the breed.

Create a Shetland Scrapbook.
Cut out pictures of different Shetland ponies. Highlight some prizewinners. Write down any facts you find about them.

Get up close.
Some summer camps have horses and ponies. Maybe one near you has Shetlands. See if you can be a camper there. Or ask your parents if you can take riding lessons. This costs a lot less than buying a pony.

Shetland ponies are a joy. Maybe you'll spend some time with these terrific animals. Or maybe you'll just learn more about them. Either way, you can't lose. You're sure to have fun.

Let's Go!

Ever watch a pony in motion? Ponies move in different ways. The ways ponies move are called gaits.

Walking is the slowest gait. The pony lifts one foot at a time off the ground. **A** trot is quicker than a walk. The pony moves two of its legs ahead at the same time. **A** canter is even speedier than a trot. The canter is a three-beat gait. Galloping is the fastest gait of all. **A** gallop feels like a very fast canter.

GLOSSARY

bay: deep red

breed: a particular type of pony. Ponies of the same breed have the same body shape and general features.

chestnut: dark reddish brown

full board: an arrangement in which a pony owner pays staff at a stable to feed and care for the pony

gait: a word to describe a pony's movements. The four gaits are walk, trot, canter, and gallop.

groom: to brush and clean a pony

horn: a knob at the front of a Western-style saddle

pit pony: a pony that hauls coal in a coal mine

tack: a pony's gear, including its saddle, reins, and bridle

FOR MORE INFORMATION

Brecke, Nicole, and Patricia M. Stockland. *Horses You Can Draw.* Minneapolis: Millbrook Press, 2010. Especially designed for horse lovers, this colorful book shows young readers how to draw different kinds of horses.

Horsefun
http://www.horsefun.com
This website is all about kids and horses. You'll find lots of horsey quizzes, puzzles, and games here. The site also features handy hints for young riders.

Landau, Elaine. *Your Pet Pony.* New York: Children's Press, 2007. This is a good guide for young people on what it takes to own and care for a pony.

McDaniel. Lurlene. *A Horse for Mandy.*
Minneapolis: Darby Creek, 2004. On her thirteenth birthday, Mandy gets her dream gift—a horse of her own. But will Mandy and her horse be able to save her best friend when tragedy strikes?

Rumsch, BreAnn. *Shetland Ponies.* Edina, MN: Abdo, 2011. Read more about the Shetland pony's looks and personality.

Silverman, Buffy. *Can You Tell a Horse from a Pony?* Minneapolis: Lerner Publications Company, 2012. Learn all about the differences between horses and ponies in this interesting book.

LERNER *e* SOURCE™

Expand learning beyond the printed book. Download free, complementary educational resources for this book from our website, www.lerneresource.com.

INDEX